DEFENCE AGAINST BRITISH GANGSTER METHODS:

SILENT KILLING

ABWEHR ENGLISCHER GANGSTER-METHODEN

«SILENT KILLING»

STILLES TÖTEN

DEFENCE AGAINST BRITISH GANGSTER METHODS:

SILENT KILLING

AOK NORWAY 1c

Images by: PK of the AOK Norway

ABWEHR ENGLISCHER GANGSTERMETHODEN

«SILENT KILLING»

STILLES TÖTEN

A. O. K. NORWEGEN I c

AUFNAHMEN: P. K. DES A. O. K.
NORWEGEN

Published by

The Naval & Military Press Ltd
Unit 5 Riverside, Brambleside
Bellbrook Industrial Estate
Uckfield, East Sussex
TN22 1QQ England

Tel: +44 (0)1825 749494

www.naval-military-press.com
www.nmarchive.com

This book is published strictly for historical purposes. The Naval and Military Press Ltd expressly bears no responsibility or liability of any type, to any first, second or third party, for any harm, injury or loss whatsoever.

In reprinting in facsimile from the original, any imperfections are inevitably reproduced and the quality may fall short of modern type and cartographic standards.

SILENT KILLING

The English guidance

The German Wehrmacht captured a hand-to-hand combat manual published for English sabotage training. The guide deals with the hitherto unknown English attack method of "silent killing".

The purpose of this type of English attack is to "surprise sentries" with the aim of "killing the enemy as quickly as possible; after all, prisoners are a burden". In the captured instructions, it also states: "If circumstances allow, kill the prisoner first, as this makes it easier to search him". This concept of silent killing was previously unknown in the German Wehrmacht. By challenging the basest instincts of the subhuman, this manual teaches how to incapacitate – or even kill – a human in an instant by strangling, slashing the eyes, kicking the head and sensitive parts of the body, and breaking the spine.

Attack types

The opponent's attack types can be categorised as follows:

I. *Armed attacks:*

    1) Knife stabs (Fig. 1-7)
    2) Pistol attacks (Fig. 8-9)
    3) Bayonet attacks (Fig. 10)

II. *Unarmed Attacks:*

    1) Choke holds (Fig. 11-17)
    2) Grappling (Fig. 18-22)
    3) Knife-edge hand strikes (Fig. 23-27)
    4) Hand strikes (Fig. 28-35)

«SILENT KILLING»

(Stilles Töten)

Die englische Vorschrift.

Eine in englischen Sabotageschulen herausgebrachte Anleitung zum Nahkampf wurde von der deutschen Wehrmacht erbeutet. Die Anleitung behandelt die bisher unbekannte englische Angriffsmethode «Silent killing», d. h. auf deutsch «stilles Töten».

Der Zweck dieser englischen Angriffsart ist, «Posten zu überrumpeln» mit dem Ziel, «den Gegner so schnell wie möglich zu töten; denn Gefangene sind nur eine Belastung». In der erbeuteten Anleitung heisst es weiter wörtlich: «Wenn die Umstände es erlauben, so töte den Gefangenen zuerst, weil es dann leichter ist, ihn zu durchsuchen». Dieses System des stillen Tötens war bisher in der deutschen Wehrmacht unbekannt. Unter Herausforderung der niedrigsten Instinkte des Untermenschen wird hier gelehrt, einen Menschen durch Erdrosselung, Hieb gegen die Augen, Fusstritte gegen Kopf und empfindliche Teile des Körpers und Brechen des Rückgrates im Nu kampfunfähig zu machen, wenn nicht gar zu töten.

Angriffsarten.

Die Angriffsarten des Gegners lassen sich, wie folgt, unterscheiden:

I. *Angriffe mit Waffen:*

    1) Messerstiche (Abb. 1—7).
    2) Pistolenangriffe (Abb. 8—9).
    3) Bajonettangriffe (Abb. 10).

II. *Angriffe ohne Waffen:*

    1) Würgegriffe (Abb. 11—17).
    2) Umklammerungen (Abb. 18—22).
    3) Handkantenschläge (Abb. 23—27).
    4) Handstösse (Abb. 28—35).

Defence

In the following, the main English stealth methods are outlined alongside the corresponding effective *defensive measures*, all demonstrated in pictures. Every defensive move should be followed by a *counterattack*, if possible.

The defensive moves stem from military close combat training and the martial art of judo.

Instructions for individual training

The training courses should last about 10 hours and be based on demonstrations by suitable athletes in the unit. To practise the individual defensive methods, puppets (stuffed sacks or old uniforms) can be used. Each hour of exercise starts with gymnastics, beginning with loosening exercises. The participants must be kept in constant motion. Each strength exercise must be followed by a relaxation exercise (see H. Dv. 475).

Special exercises include: jumping in a squat, quick turns in a deep squat (all exercises done while on tiptoe), the duck walk in a deep squat, and balancing exercises in pairs. Next, practise hardening the knife-edges of your hands on table edges, and strengthening your fingertips by "drumming" on hard objects.

Abwehr.

Im folgenden werden die hauptsächlichen englischen Überfallmethoden bekanntgegeben und entsprechende wirkungsvolle *Abwehrmassnahmen* im Bilde gezeigt. Jedem Abwehrgriff soll nach Möglichkeit der *Gegenangriff* folgen.

Die Abwehrgriffe stammen aus der militärischen Nahkampfausbildung und dem Yudo-Kampfsport.

Anleitung zum Selbstüben.

Die Vorbereitungskurse sollen sich auf etwa 10 Stunden erstrecken und auf Vorführungen geeigneter Sportler in der Einheit aufbauen. Zum Üben der einzelnen Abwehrgriffe verwendet man zweckmässig Puppen (ausgestopfte Säcke oder alte Uniformen). Jede Übungsstunde beginnt mit Gymnastik, dabei zunächst Lockerungsübungen. Die Teilnehmer sind ständig in Bewegung zu halten. Jeder Kraftübung muss wieder eine Lockerungsübung folgen (siehe H. Dv. 475).

Besondere Übungen sind: In der Kniebeuge hüpfen, schnelle Drehungen in tiefer Hocke (alle Übungen auf den Zehenspitzen stehend), der Entengang in tiefer Hocke und Gleichgewichtsübungen zu zweit. Weiter übe man das Abhärten der Handkanten an Tischkanten und stärke die Fingerspitzen durch «Trommeln» auf harten Gegenständen.

Armed Attacks

DEFENCE: **COUNTER-ATTACK:**

Knife stabs (Fig. 1-7).

a) Knife stabs from the front, from above, in the shoulder (Fig. 1-3):

    Double-armed high defensive cover

    or

    Intercepting the stabbing arm

    Kick the attacker's shin

    or

    Knife-edge hand hit to attacker's upper lip

    or

    Knife-edge hand hits and kicks against the attacker

b) Knife stab from the front, from below (Fig. 4-5)

    Double-armed low defensive cover

    Kick the attacker's shin

c) Knife stab from behind, in the neck (Fig. 6)

    Crouch down and try to get out of attacker's reach

    "Donkey kick", kick to the attacker's shin or knee

d) Defence when prone (Fig. 7)

    Curl up, two-armed cover

    Kick the attacker's shins, knees, abdomen, or stomach

Angriffe mit Waffen.

ABWEHR: **GEGENANGRIFF:**

1) Messerstiche (Abb. 1—7).

a) Messerstich von vorn hoch, in die Schulter (Abb. 1—3):

ABWEHR	GEGENANGRIFF
beidarmige Deckung hoch *oder* Abfangen des stechenden Armes.	Tritt gegen das Schienbein des Angreifers *oder* Handkantenhieb gegen die Oberlippe des Angreifers *oder* Handkantenhieb und Fusstritte gegen den Angreifer.

b) Messerstich von vorn tief (Abb. 4—5):

ABWEHR	GEGENANGRIFF
Beidarmige Deckung tief.	Tritt gegen das Schienbein des Angreifers.

c) Messerstich von hinten, in den Hals (Abb. 6):

ABWEHR	GEGENANGRIFF
Nach unten wegducken und versuchen, aus der Reichweite des Angreifers zu kommen.	Nach hinten «auskeilen», Tritt gegen das Schienbein oder Knie des Angreifers.

d) Abwehr im Liegen (Abb. 7).

ABWEHR	GEGENANGRIFF
Zusammenrollen, beidarmige Deckung.	Tritte gegen das Schienbein, Knie, den Unterleib oder Magen des Angreifers.

Pistol attacks (Fig. 8-9)

Pistol attacks from the front (Fig. 8-9)

    Jump to the side   Hit the attacker on the chin to make him fall

Bayonet attacks (Fig. 10)

a) Bayonet attack from the front (Fig. 10):

    Jump to the side   Kick at or against the weapon

2) Pistolenangriffe (Abb. 8—9).

a) Pistolenangriff von vorn (Abb. 8—9):

Zur Seite springen.   Durch Schlag gegen die Kinnpartie den Angreifer zu Fall bringen.

3) Bajonettangriffe (Abb. 10).

a) Bajonettangriff von vorn (Abb. 10):

Zur Seite springen.   Tritt gegen oder auf das Gewehr.

Unarmed Attacks

| DEFENCE | COUNTERATTACK |

1) Choke Holds (Fig. 11-17)

a) Two-handed choke hold from the rear: (Fig. 11-12a):

Immediately pull your chin down towards your neck, prise apart the attacker's fingers	Kick the attacker's instep, ankle, shin or knee

b) Two-handed choke hold from the front (Fig. 13-15):

Immediately pull your chin deep into your neck, raise your hands, clasp them together and quickly punch them down	Kick the attacker's abdomen.
or	or
Push off the opponent's arm	Thrust the base of the palm into the attacker's upper lip

2) Grappling (Fig. 18-22)

a) Grappling from the rear (Fig. 18-19)

Dodge by squatting, hitting the opponent's head with your steel helmet, prising apart their hands	Donkey kick to the rear, kicking the attacker's instep, shin, or knee

Angriffe ohne Waffen.

ABWEHR:	GEGENANGRIFF:

1) Würgegriffe (Abb. 11—17).

a) **Beidhändiger Würgegriff von hinten:** (Abb. 11—12 a):

Kinn sofort tief an den Hals heranziehen. Finger aufreissen.	Tritt gegen den Spann, Knöchel, das Schienbein oder Knie des Angreifers.

b) **Beidhändiger Würgegriff von vorn** (Abb. 13—15):

Kinn sofort tief an den Hals heranziehen, Hände hochreissen, ineinanderfassen und schnell nach unten durchschlagen *oder* Abdrängen des gegnerischen Armes.	Tritt gegen den Unterleib des Angreifers *oder* Handballenhieb gegen die Oberlippe des Angreifers.

c) **Einhändiger Würgegriff von vorn** (Abb.. 16—17):

Kinn sofort tief an den Hals heranziehen, aus dem Griff herausdrehen.	Tritt nach vorn gegen das Schienbein, Knie oder den Unterleib des Angreifers.

2) Umklammerungen (Abb. 18—22).

a) **Umklammerungen von hinten** (Abb. 18—19):

Wegducken durch Kniebeuge, Schlag mit dem Stahlhelm nach dem Kopf des Gegners, Hände aufreissen.	Nach hinten «auskeilen», Tritt gegen Spann, Schienbein oder Knie des Angreifers.

DEFENCE	COUNTERATTACK

b) Grappling from the front (Fig. 20-22)

Press both arms sideways to force off the attacker's arms, then duck away by bending your knees	Kick the attacker's instep or (Fig. 20)
	Knee to the abdomen and kick to the attacker's shin
	Or with free arms (fig. 20) punch the attacker's abdomen
	Or with free arms (Fig. 21) thumb screw behind the ears.
Push off the opponent's arm	Hit the attacker's chin to knock him down (Fig. 22)
	or
	Finger jabs to attacker's neck and eyes

3) Knife-edge hand strikes (Fig. 23-25).

a) Knife-edge hand strike to the head (Fig. 23-25).

Two-armed defensive cover	Knife-edge hand hits against the attacker's head and neck, as well as kicks

ABWEHR:	GEGENANGRIFF:
b) Umklammerungen von vorn (Abb. 20—22):	
Mit kräftigem Druck beide Arme seitwärts heben und so die Arme des Angreifers abstreifen, wegducken durch Kniebeuge.	Fusstritt auf den Spann des Angreifers oder (Abb. 20) Kniestoss gegen den Unterleib und Fusstritt gegen das Schienbein des Angreifers oder bei freien Armen (Abb. 20) Fausthieb gegen den Unterleib des Angreifers oder bei freien Armen (Abb. 21) Daumenschraube hinter den Ohren.
Abdrängen eines gegnerischen Armes	Durch Schlag gegen die Kinnpartie den Angreifer zu Fall bringen (Abb. 22) oder Fingerstösse gegen den Hals und die Augen des Angreifers.

3) Handkantenschläge (Abb. 23—25).

a) Handkantenschläge gegen den Kopf (Abb. 23—25):

ABWEHR:	GEGENANGRIFF:
Beidarmige Deckung hoch	Handkantenhiebe gegen den Kopf und Hals des Angreifers, Fusstritte austeilen.

DEFENCE	COUNTERATTACK
b)	(Fig. 26-27):
Double-armed defensive cover against the opponent's punching arm	Knife-edge hand hits against the attacker's head and neck, as well as kicks

4) Finger and hand jabs (Fig. 28.35)

a) Finger jab to the eyes (Fig. 28-29):

Hold your hand vertically in front of your face	Kick the sensitive parts of the attacker's body

b) Finger jab to the neck (Fig. 30-32):

Double-armed high defensive cover, hit the attacking arm to the side	Knife-edge hand hits and finger jabs to the attacker's head

c) Hand jab from below (Fig. 33-35):

Double-armed low defensive cover	Kick the opponent's shins, knees or abdomen

ABWEHR:	GEGENANGRIFF:
b)	(Abb. 26—27):
Einarmige Deckung gegen den schlagenden Arm des Gegners.	Handkantenhiebe gegen den Kopf und Hals des Angreifers. Fusstritte austeilen.

4) Finger- und Handstösse (Abb. 28—35).

a) Fingerstoss gegen die Augen (Abb. 28—29):

Hand senkrecht vor das Gesicht halten.	Fusstritte gegen empfindliche Körperteile des Angreifers.

b) Fingerstoss gegen den Hals (Abb. 30—32):

Beidarmige Deckung hoch, den stossenden Arm zur Seite schlagen.	Handkantenhiebe und Fingerstösse gegen Kopf des Angreifers.

c) Handstoss tief (Abb. 33—35):

Beidarmige Deckung tief.	Tritt gegen Schienbein, Knie oder Unterleib des Gegners.

DEFENCE AGAINST BRITISH GANGSTER METHODS:

SILENT KILLING

ABWEHR ENGLISCHER GANGSTERMETHODEN

«SILENT KILLING»
STILLES TÖTEN

Fig. 1

Attack: Knife stab from the front, from above, in the shoulder.

Defence: Double-armed high defensive cover (see Fig. 24).

Counterattack: Kick the attacker's shin (right).

Abb. 1

Angriff: Messerstich von vorn hoch, in die Schulter.

Abwehr: Beidarmige Deckung hoch (siehe Abb. 24).
Gegenangriff: Tritt gegen das Schienbein des Angreifers (rechts).

Fig. 2

Attack: Knife stab from the front, from above.

Defence: Block the attacking arm.

Counterattack: Knife-edge hand hit to the attacker's upper lip (right).

Abb. 2

Angriff: Messerstich von vorn hoch.

Abwehr: Abfangen des stechenden Armes.
Gegenangriff: Handkantenhieb gegen die Oberlippe des Angreifers (rechts).

Fig. 3

Attack: Knife stab from the front, from above, in the shoulder.

Defence: Double-armed high defensive cover.

Counterattack: Knife-edge hand hits as well as kicks to the attacker (right).

Abb. 3

Angriff: Messerstich von vorn hoch, in die Schulter.

Abwehr: Beidarmige Deckung hoch.
Gegenangriff: Handkantenhiebe und Fusstritte gegen den Angreifer (rechts).

Fig. 4

Attack: Knife stab from the front, from below.
Defence: Double-armed low defensive cover.
Counterattack: Kicks to the attacker's shin (right).

Abb. 4

Angriff: Messerstich von vorn tief.

Abwehr: Beidarmige Deckung tief.
Gegenangriff: Tritt gegen das Schienbein des Angreifers (rechts).

Fig. 5

Attack: Knife stab from the front, from below.

Defence: Two-armed low defensive cover.

Counterattack: Kick the attacker's shin (right).

Abb. 5

Angriff: Messerstich von vorn tief.

Abwehr: Beidarmige Deckung tief.
Gegenangriff: Tritt gegen das Schienbein des Angreifers (rechts).

Fig. 6

Attack: Knife stab from behind, in the neck.

Defence: Duck down and try to get out of attacker's reach.

Counterattack: "Donkey kick" to the rear, kick the attacker's shin or knee.

Abb. 6

Angriff: Messerstich von hinten, in den Hals.

Abwehr: Nach unten wegducken und versuchen, aus der Reichweite des Angreifers zu kommen.
Gegenangriff: Nach hinten «auskeilen», Tritt gegen das Schienbein oder Knie des Angreifers.

Fig. 7

Defence: Roll up, two-armed cover.

Counterattack: Kick the attacker's shins, knees, abdomen or stomach.

Abb. 7

Abwehr: Zusammenrollen, beidarmige Deckung.
Gegenangriff: Tritte gegen das Schienbein, Knie, den Unterleib oder Magen des Angreifers.

Fig. 8

Attack: Pistol attack from the front.

Defence: Jump to the side.

Counterattack: Trip up the attacker (right) by sticking out a leg, then hit him on the chin.

Abb. 8

Angriff: Pistolenangriff von vorn.

Abwehr: Zur Seite springen.
Gegenangriff: Durch «Beinchen stellen» und Schlag gegen die Kinnpartie den Angreifer (rechts) zu Fall bringen.

Fig. 9

Attack: Pistol attack from the front.

Defence: Jump to the side.

Counterattack: Trip up the attacker by sticking out a leg, then hit him on the head.

Abb. 9

Angriff: Pistolenangriff von vorn.

Abwehr: Zur Seite springen.
Gegenangriff: Durch «Beinchen stellen» und Schlag gegen den Kopf den Gegner zu Fall bringen.

Fig. 10

Attack: Bayonet attack from the front.

Defence: Jump to the side.
Counterattack: Kick against or on the weapon.

In this attack, the weapon is usually held horizontally or tilted downwards. A quick kick to the weapon throws them off balance. Counterattack immediately.

Abb. 10

Angriff: Bajonettangriff von vorn.

Abwehr: Zur Seite springen.

Gegenangriff: Tritt gegen oder auf das Gewehr.

Bei diesem Angriff wird das Gewehr meist horizontal oder nach unten geneigt geführt. Ein schneller Tritt gegen die Waffe bringt sie aus der Stossrichtung. Sofort zum Gegenangriff übergehen.

Fig. 11

Attack: Two-handed choke hold from behind.

Defence: See next page.

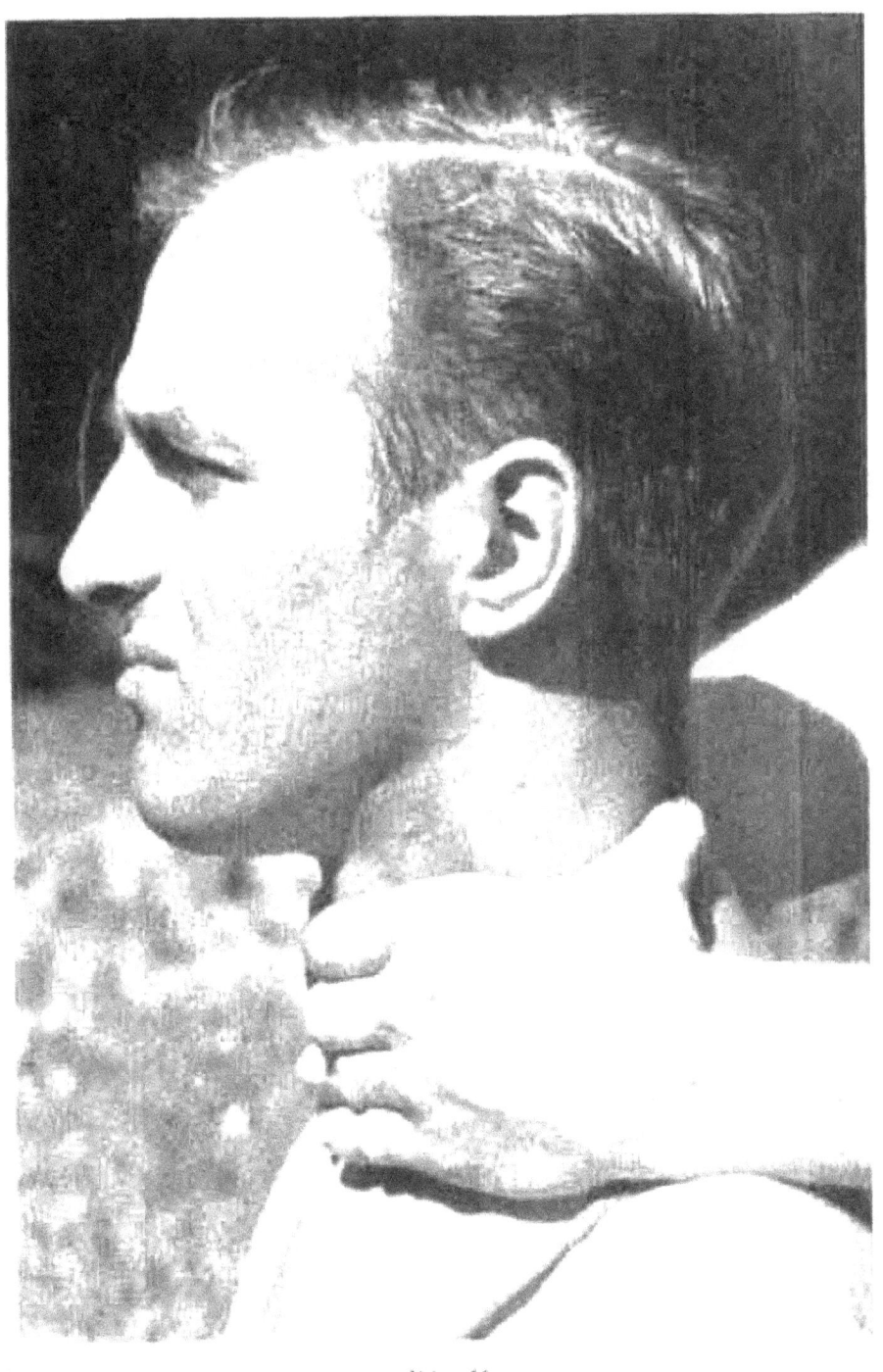

Abb. 11

Angriff: Beidhändiger Würgegriff von hinten.

Abwehr: Siehe nächste Seite.

Fig. 12

Defence: Immediately pull your chin deep into your neck, prise apart your opponent's hands, pull apart the little fingers with a strong grip.

Counterattack: Back kick against attacker's instep, ankle, shin or knee (right).

Abb. 12

Abwehr: Kinn sofort tief an den Hals heranziehen, Hände des Gegners aufreissen, die kleinen Finger mit starkem Griff wegspreizen.

Gegenangriff: Tritt nach hinten gegen den Spann, Knöchel, das Schienbein oder Knie des Angreifers (rechts).

Fig. 12a

Attack: Two-handed choke hold from the rear.

Defence: When prising apart the little finger, bend the attacker's little finger outwards with a strong jerk.

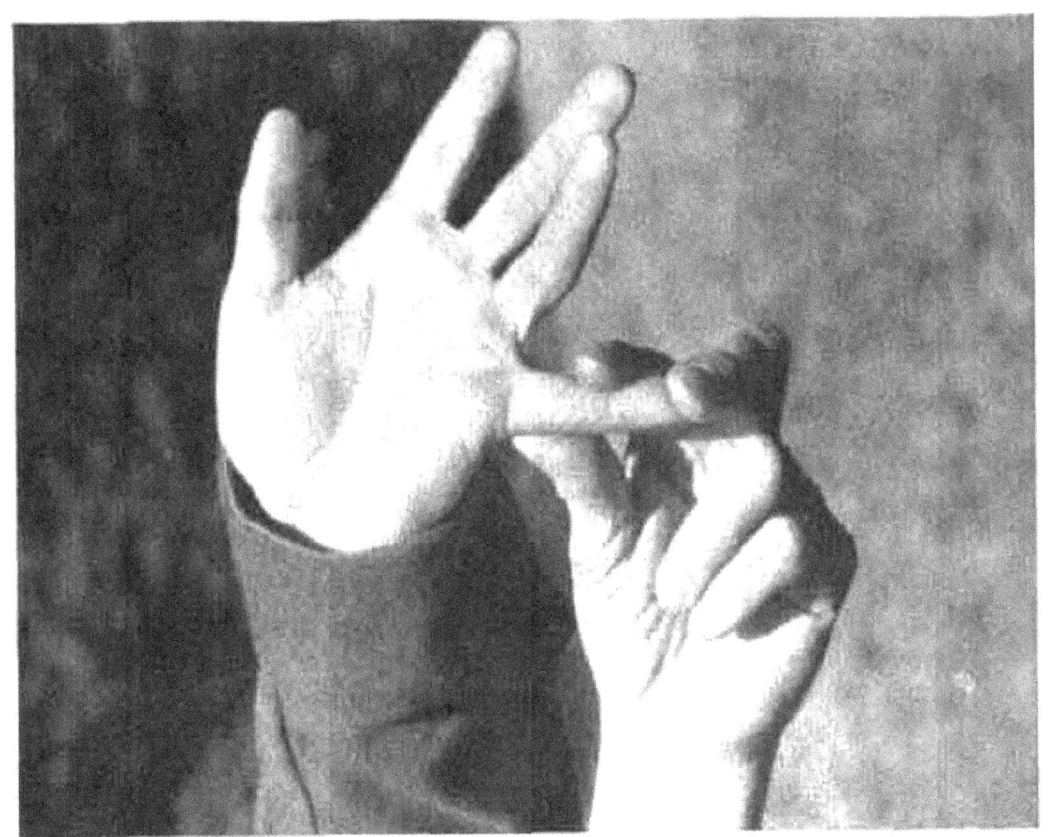

Abb. 12a

Angriff: Beidhändiger Würgegriff von hinten.

Abwehr: Beim Wegspreizen des kleinen Fingers biegt man den kleinen Finger des Angreifers mit kräftigem Ruck nach aussen.

Fig. 13

Attack: Two-handed choke hold from the front.

Defence: Page 25. Fig. 14

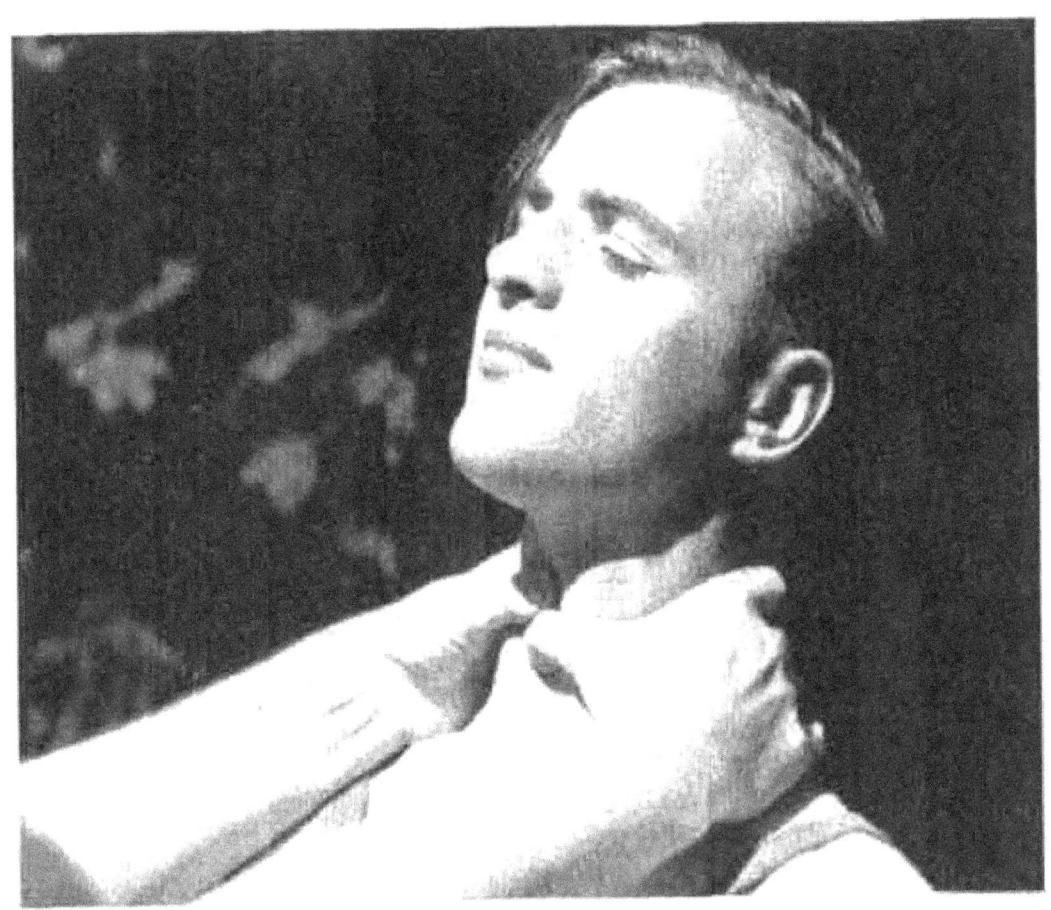

Abb. 13

Angriff: Beidhändiger Würgegriff von vorn.

Abwehr: Seite 25, Abb. 14.

Fig. 14

Defence: Immediately pull your chin down towards your neck. Force your hands up, clasp them and quickly punch down.

Counterattack: Kick the opponent's abdomen.

Abb. 14

Abwehr: Kinn sofort tief an den Hals heranziehen, Hände hochreissen, ineinanderfassen und schnell nach unten durchschlagen.

Gegenangriff: Tritt gegen den Unterleib des Gegners.

Fig. 14a

Attack: Two-handed choke hold from the front.

Defence: Raise your hands, clasp them together and punch down quickly.

Counterattack: Knee into the attacker's abdomen or kick the instep or shin.

Abb. 14 a

Angriff: Beidhändiger Würgegriff von vorn.

Abwehr: Hände hochreissen, ineinanderfassen und schnell nach unten durchschlagen.

Gegenangriff: Mit dem Knie Stoss gegen den Unterleib des Angreifers oder Tritt gegen Rist oder Schienbein.

Fig. 15

Attack: Two-handed choke hold from the front.

Defence: Force away the opponent's arm.

Counterattack: Knife-edge hand hit to the attacker's upper lip (right).

Abb. 15

Angriff: Beidhändiger Würgegriff von vorn.

Abwehr: Abdrängen des gegnerischen Armes.
Gegenangriff: Handballenhieb gegen die Oberlippe des Angreifers (rechts).

Fig. 16

Attack: One-handed choke hold from the front.

Defence: Page 29, fig. 17.

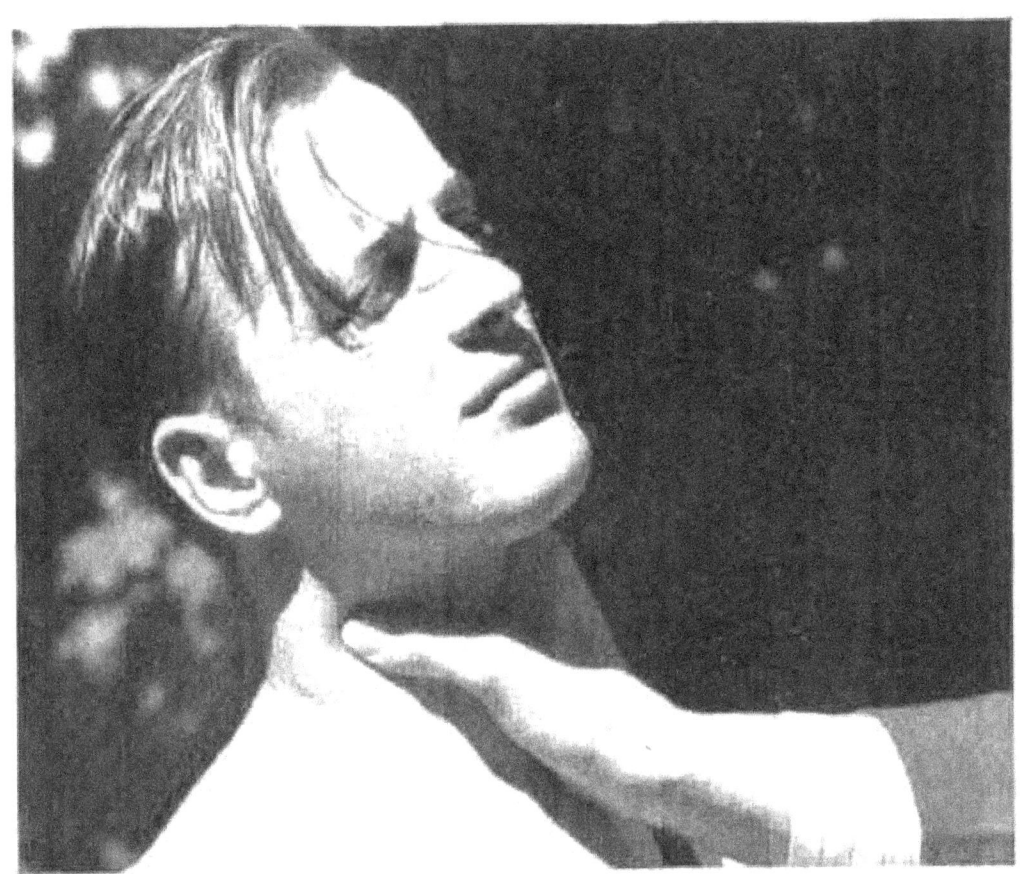

Abb. 16

Angriff: Einhändiger Würgegriff von vorn.

Abwehr: Seite 29, Abb. 17.

Fig. 17

Defence: Immediately pull your chin low against your neck and twist it out of the attacker's grip.

Counterattack: Kick forward at the attacker's shins, knees or abdomen.

Abb. 17

Abwehr: Kinn sofort tief an den Hals heranziehen und aus dem Griff herausdrehen.
Gegenangriff: Tritt nach vorn gegen das Schienbein, Knie oder den Unterleib des Angreifers.

Fig. 18

Attack: Grapple from the rear.

Defence: Duck away by bending the knees, then hit the attacker's head with your steel helmet (right).

Counterattack: "Donkey kick" to the rear, then kicks against attacker's instep, shin or knee.

Abb. 18

Angriff: Umklammerung von hinten.

Abwehr: Wegducken durch Kniebeuge. Schlag mit dem Stahlhelm nach dem Kopf des Angreifers (rechts).

Gegenangriff: Nach hinten «auskeilen». Tritt gegen Spann, Schienbein oder Knie des Angreifers.

Fig. 19

Attack: Grapple from behind.

Defence: Prise apart the attacker's hands, duck away by bending your knees.

Counterattack: Kick against the attacker's instep

Abb. 19

Angriff: Umklammerung von hinten.

Abwehr: Hände aufreissen, Wegducken durch Kniebeuge.

Gegenangriff: Tritt auf den Spann des Angreifers.

Fig. 20

Attack: Grapple from the front.

Defence: Force up both arms to the side to release the attacker's grip, then duck away by bending your knees.

Counterattack: Kick the attacker's instep.

Abb. 20

Angriff: Umklammerung von vorn.

Abwehr: Mit kräftigem Druck beide Arme seitwärts nach oben heben und so die Arme des Angreifers abstreifen, wegducken durch Kniebeuge.
Gegenangriff: Fusstritt auf den Spann des Angreifers.

Fig. 20a

Attack: Grapple from the front

Defence: Force up both arms to the side to release the attacker's grip.

Counterattack: Knee to attacker's abdomen, kick to shin.

Abb. 20 a

Angriff: Umklammerung von vorn.

Abwehr: Mit kräftigem Druck beide Arme seitwärts nach oben heben und so die Arme des Angreifers abstreifen.

Gegenangriff: Kniestoss gegen den Unterleib des Angreifers, Fusstritt gegen Schienbein.

Fig. 20b

Attack: Grapple from the front, arms left free.

Defence: Evade by squatting.

Counterattack: Punch the attacker's abdomen.

Abb. 20 b

Angriff: Umklammerung von vorn, Arme frei.

Abwehr: Wegducken durch Kniebeuge.
Gegenangriff: Fausthieb gegen den Unterleib des Angreifers.

Fig. 21

Attack: Grapple from the front, arms left free.

Defence: Thumbscrew move behind the attacker's ears: Press your thumbs firmly into the hollows on the attacker's head, behind their ears.

Abb. 21

Angriff: Umklammerung von vorn. Arme frei.

Abwehr: Daumenschraube hinter den Ohren des Angreifers:

Man drückt seine Daumen kräftig in die Höhlungen am Kopfe hinter den Ohrmuscheln.

Fig. 22

Attack: Grapple from the front.

Defence: Push off the attacker's arms.

Counterattack: Hit the attacker in the jaw to make them fall, or finger jab the attacker in the neck and eyes.

Abb. 22

Angriff: Umklammerung von vorn.

Abwehr: Abdrängen eines gegnerischen Armes.
Gegenangriff: Durch Schlag gegen die Kinnpartie den Angreifer zu Fall bringen oder Fingerstösse gegen Hals und Augen des Angreifers.

Fig. 23

Attack: The deadly knife-edge hand hit against the carotid artery.
Defence: p. 40, fig. 24

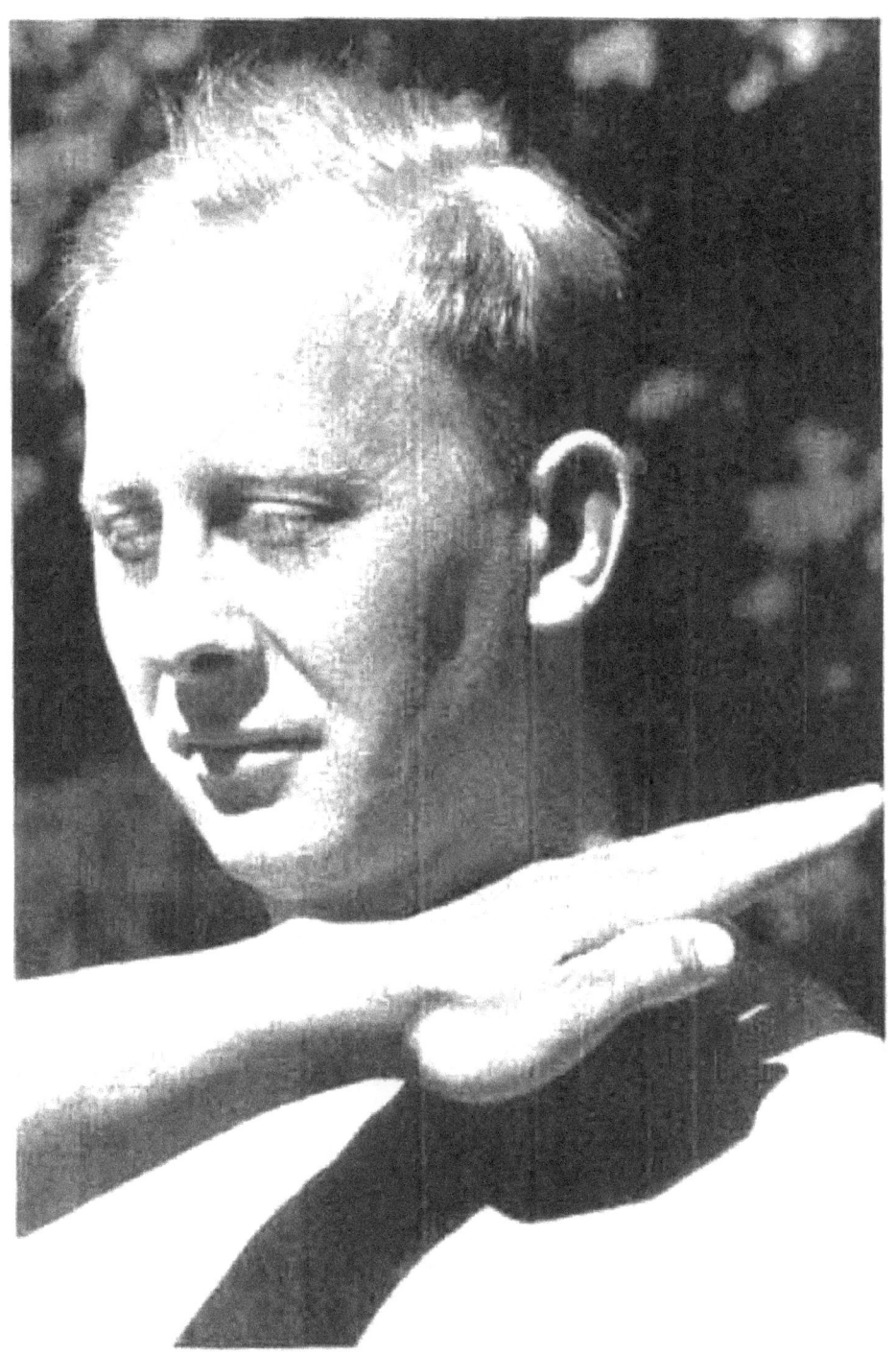

Abb. 23

Angriff: Der tödliche Handkantenhieb gegen die Halsschlagader.

Abwehr: S. 40, Abb. 24.

Fig. 23a

Attack: The deadly knife-edge hand hit to the temple
Defence: p. 40. Fig. 24.

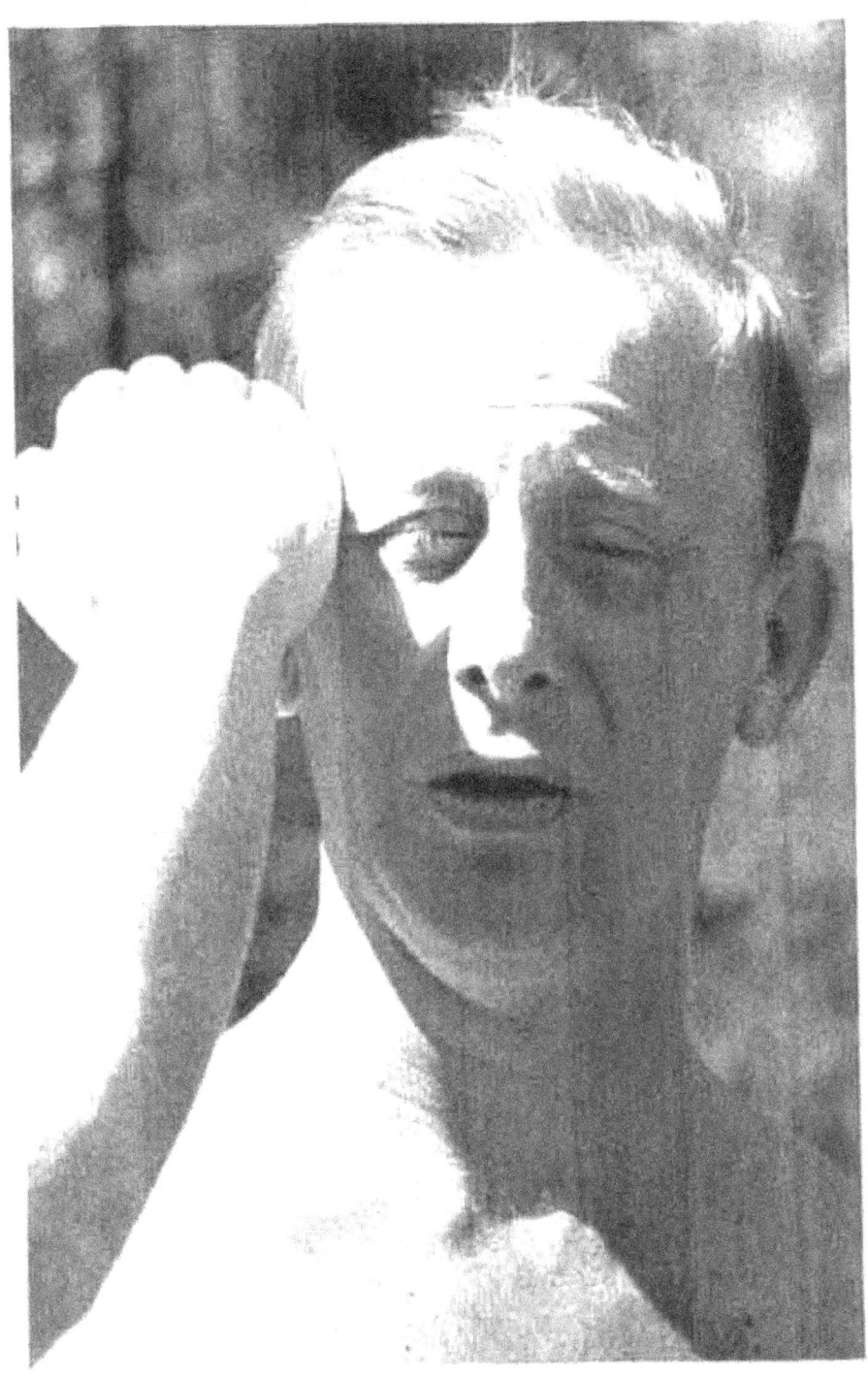

Abb. 23 a

Angriff: Der tödliche Handkantenhieb gegen die Schläfe.

Abwehr: S. 40, Abb. 24.

Fig. 23b

Attack: The deadly knife-edge hand hit to the upper lip

Defence: p. 40. Fig. 24

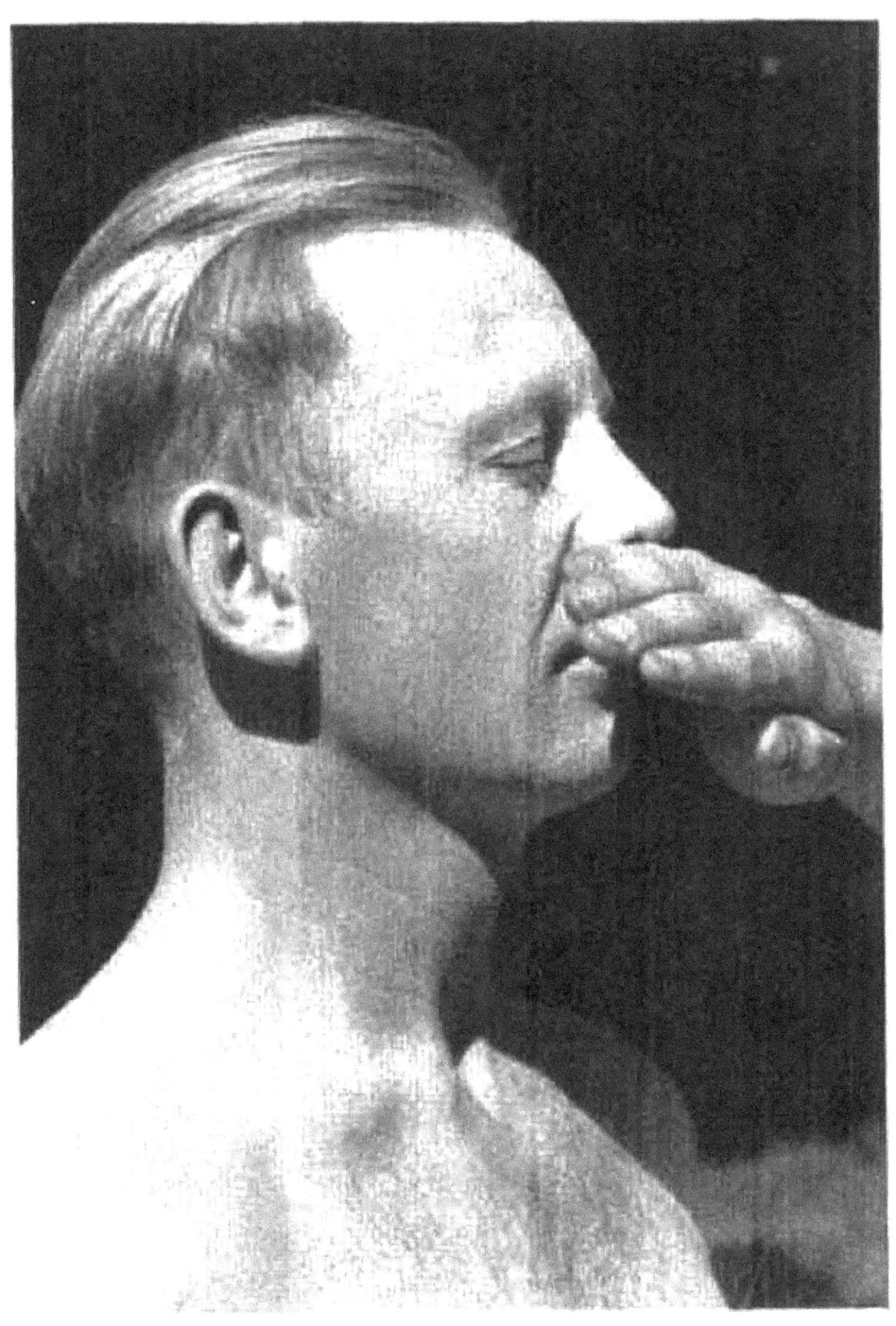

Abb. 23 b

Angriff: Der tödliche Handkantenhieb gegen die Oberlippe.

Abwehr: S. 40, Abb. 24.

Fig. 24

Defence: Proper hand defensive position against jabs and blows to the head (both-armed high defensive cover).

This stance leads to a later counterattack of knife-edge hand jabs against the attacker's head or neck.

Abb. 24

Abwehr: Richtige Handabwehrstellung gegen Hiebe und Stösse gegen den Kopf (beidarmige Deckung hoch).

Aus dieser Haltung ergibt sich der spätere Gegenangriff mit Handkantenhieben gegen den Kopf oder Hals des Angreifers.

Fig. 25

Attack: Knife-edge hand hits to the head or neck.

Defence: Two-armed high defensive cover.

Counterattack: Knife-edge hand jabs to the attacker's head and neck, as well as kicks.

This defensive cover absorbs any blows to the head. Note the coiled nature of the defensive pose (left), which allows for lightning-fast evasion in any direction.

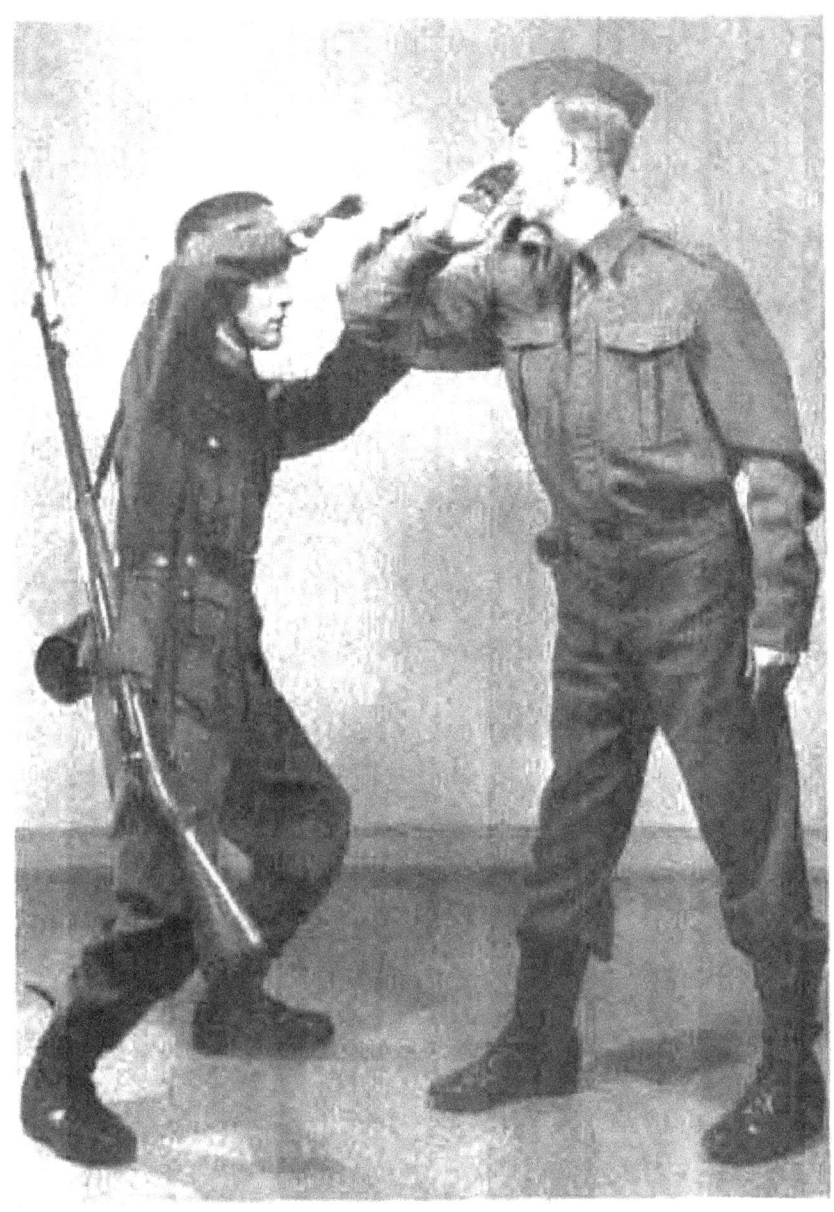

Abb. 25

Angriff: Handkantenhieb gegen den Kopf oder Hals.

Abwehr: Beidarmige Deckung hoch.

Gegenangriff: Handkantenhiebe gegen den Kopf und Hals des Angreifers, Fusstritte austeilen.
Diese Deckung fängt jeden Schlag gegen den Kopf ab. Beachte die federnde Stellung des abwehrenden Postens (links), die ein blitzschnelles Ausweichen nach jeder Richtung ermöglicht.

Fig. 26 and 26a

Defence: Proper one-armed defensive cover against jabs and blows to the head. Note the stretched edge of the hand, which becomes a bludgeoning weapon in a *counterattack*.

Abb. 26 und 26 a

Abwehr: Richtige einarmige Abwehrstellung gegen Hiebe und Stösse gegen den Kopf. Beachte die gestreckte Handkante, die in Gegenangriff zur Schlagwaffe wird.

Fig. 27

Attack: Knife-edge hand hit to the neck.

Defence: One-armed defensive cover against the attacker's punching arm.

Counterattack: Knife-edge hand hit to the attacker's head and neck, kicks to shins or knees.

Abb. 27

Angriff: Handkantenhieb gegen den Hals.

Abwehr: Einarmige Deckung gegen den schlagenden Arm des Angreifers.
Gegenangriff: Handkantenhieb gegen den Kopf und Hals des Angreifers, Fusstritte gegen Schienbein oder Knie.

Fig 28

Attack: Finger jab to the eyes.

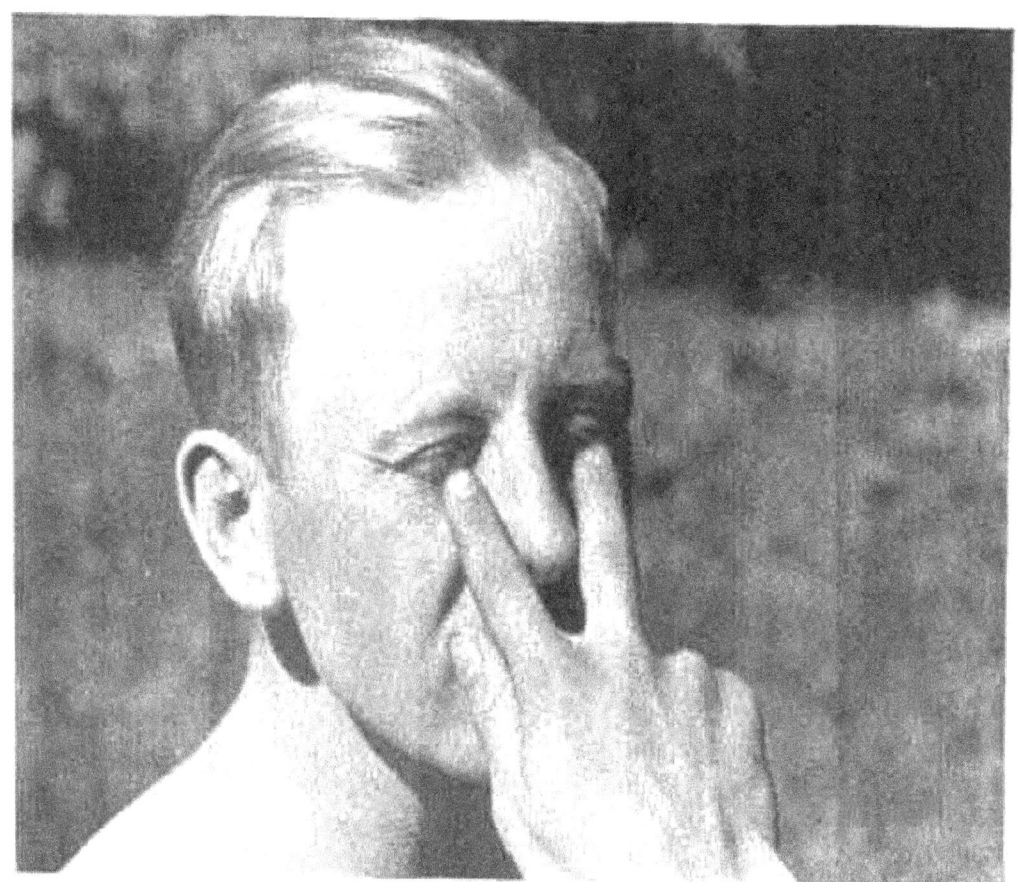
Abb. 28

Angriff: Fingerstoss gegen die Augen

Fig. 29

Defence: Hold your hand vertically in front of your face.

Counterattack: Kick against the sensitive parts of the attacker's body (right). By holding your hand vertically in front of the eyes (thumb on the nose) you can catch the attacker's finger jab, while leaving you the necessary view of your opponent.

Abb. 29

Abwehr: Hand senkrecht vor das Gesicht halten.

Gegenangriff: Fusstritte gegen empfindliche Körperteile des Angreifers (rechts). Die senkrecht vor die Augen gehaltene Hand (Daumen an der Nase) fängt den Fingerstoss auf, lässt aber gleichzeitig die notwendige Sicht auf den Gegner frei.

Fig. 30

Attack: Finger jab to the neck.

Abb. 30

Angriff: Fingerstoss gegen den Hals.

Fig. 31

Defence: Two-armed high defensive cover, push the thrusting arm to the side.

Counterattack: Knife-edge hand hits and finger jabs to the attacker's head.

Abb. 31

Abwehr: Beidarmige Deckung hoch, den stossenden Arm zur Seite schlagen.

Gegenangriff: Handkantenhiebe und Fingerstösse gegen den Kopf des Angreifers.

Fig. 32

Attack: Punch to the neck.

Defence: Two-armed high defensive cover, push the thrusting arm to the side.

Counterattack: Kick the attacker's shins or knees.

Abb. 32

Angriff: Handstoss gegen den Hals.

Abwehr: Beidarmige Deckung hoch, den stossenden Arm zur Seite schlagen.
Gegenangriff: Tritt gegen Schienbein oder Knie des Angreifers.

Fig. 33

Attack: Punches, low.

Defence: Two-armed low defensive cover.

Counterattack: Kick the attacker's shins, knees or abdomen.

Abb. 33

Angriff: Handstösse tief.

Abwehr: Beidarmige tiefe Deckung.

Gegenangriff: Tritt gegen das Schienbein, Knie oder den Unterleib des Gegners.

Fig. 34

Attack: Punches, low.

Defence: Proper two-armed defensive cover against blows aimed at the abdomen.

Abb. 34

Angriff: Handstösse tief.

Abwehr: Richtige beidarmige Abwehr gegen Schläge, die gegen den Unterleib gerichtet sind.

Fig. 35

Attack: Punch to the stomach.

Defence: Two-armed low defensive cover.

Counterattack: Kick the attacker's shins, knees or abdomen.

Abb. 35

Angriff: Fausthieb gegen den Bauch.

Abwehr: Beidarmige Deckung tief.
Gegenangriff: Tritt gegen Schienbein, Knie oder Unterleib des Angreifers.

These gangster methods are unnatural to the German soldier. Yet, we must adapt to them. Once attacked, one must defend oneself by the same means used by one's attacker.

Once you have defended yourself against an attacker, there is only one goal: to incapacitate them as quickly as possible via counterattack.

The English manual states: "Students should note that many of these grapple-holds, etc., are difficult – if not impossible – to carry out when faced with a practised opponent. And it would be exceedingly unwise to assume that the opponent is unpractised."

So, let us practise!

Diese Gangstermethoden liegen dem deutschen Soldaten wenig. Wir müssen uns aber auf sie einstellen. Einmal angefallen, wehrt man sich mit den gleichen Mitteln, mit denen man angegriffen wird.

Hat man sich des angreifenden Gegners erwehrt, dann gibt es nur ein Ziel: Den Gegner so schnell wie möglich im Gegenangriff kampfunfähig machen.

In der englischen Anleitung heisst es: «Man muss die Schüler darauf hinweisen, dass viele dieser Griffe usw. schwierig, wenn nicht gar unmöglich sind, wenn man einem geübten Gegner gegenübersteht. Und anzunehmen, dass der Gegner ungeübt ist, wäre ausserordentlich unklug.»

Ueben wir uns also!